EXTREME SCOTLAND

NADIR KHAN

EXTREME SCOTLAND

A photographic journey
through Scottish adventure sports

VP

Vertebrate Publishing, Sheffield
www.v-publishing.co.uk

NADIR KHAN
EXTREME SCOTLAND

First published in 2018 by Vertebrate Publishing.

 VERTEBRATE PUBLISHING
Crescent House, 228 Psalter Lane, Sheffield S11 8UT, United Kingdom.
www.v-publishing.co.uk

Front cover: Tom Livingstone and Uisdean Hawthorn on *Pic 'n' Mix* (VIII, 8), Coire an Lochain, Cairngorms.
Back cover: Guy Stevens and Lee Fleming on Sgùrr Alasdair, Isle of Skye.

A CIP catalogue record for this book is available from the British Library.

ISBN: 978-1-911342-90-8 (Hardback)

10 9 8 7 6 5 4 3 2 1

Design and production by Jane Beagley.

www.v-publishing.co.uk

Vertebrate Publishing is committed to printing on paper from sustainable sources.

Printed and bound in Europe by Latitude Press Ltd.

CONTENTS

FOREWORD

Over the years I have had endless discussions with film colleagues as to which medium stands up best to the ravages of time: the powerful and instantaneous impact of the moving picture, or the timeless book.

My choice is the book of words or illustrations, and I must admit I am a large-format buff, an admirer of Vittorio Sella and the Abraham brothers – such subtle light and shadows!

But with the move to the digital medium away from slide and print film, there is a blurring of the lines between reality, enhanced reality and fantasy. Honesty can become something of a scarce commodity in the modern age of instant fixes to our digital life. But artists have always sought to try and augment their images: whether it be Ansel Adams and the use of filters or the saturated colours of slide film or creating composites from a number of images in the dark room, the role of the artist photographer has always been to present a view of the world as seen through their imagination and through the lens of the camera.

In *Extreme Scotland* Nadir Khan has created a memorable work, one that is far reaching into the vast outdoors that he so clearly loves deeply. The use of the digital medium transports us to experience and feel some of the very best that Scotland has to offer. All the major outdoor disciplines are here and I'm sure his fine book will have broad appeal.

I congratulate him.

Hamish MacInnes
Glencoe

« *Climbers on* Curved Ridge (III), Buachaille Etive Mòr, in winter.

The 'ten-minute tree' on the walk in to the north face of Ben Nevis. This beautiful tree is a marker at the end of a long day on the Ben as you know you're nearly back at the car.

INTRODUCTION

Scotland is as beautiful and diverse as its inhabitants. For those of us who seek adventure in the mountains, rivers and seas, the land isn't just the physical ground upon which we walk and run and play, but an emotional pulse that beats deep within our hearts and souls.

I saw my first 'mountain' when I was four years old. My first thought was that I had to climb it and see what my world would look like from its lonely summit … 'Topping out' set alight a flame that's never been extinguished, and started my journey to rock and ice climbing, kayaking, skiing, snowboarding and kite surfing. When I discovered photography as a student at Glasgow university, it was a natural progression to begin photographing my pals as we muddled our way through early adventure and misadventure in the mountains.

That first mountain was in fact an old slag heap behind Law Hospital doctors' flats where we had moved to shortly after coming to Scotland as immigrants, my father being a surgeon at the hospital. Inspiration is found in unexpected places …

This book is a visual and lyrical celebration of all that makes Scotland special: the fickle and changeable weather, the amazing light and land-scapes, and of course the hard men and women who push themselves physically and mentally, in sometimes terrible conditions, to forge new routes, run impossible skyline ridges, and kayak and surf beautiful crystal-blue waters.

Some of the images in this book were shot while on commission for clients, some were shot when I was out with pals having our own adventures, and some were shot specifically for the book.

The photos are as much a celebration of Scotland itself – and of those wild and rugged places that touch our souls – as of its adventure sports. Some images are included just because they are beautiful images – backlit grass or autumn colours or ice formations on a river – and these are as good a reason to get outside and be inspired as those of climbing or running or skiing.

As well as the photography there are some pieces from writers and poets that reflect the diverse conditions and emotions that are experienced in the mountains. Adventure is only part of a bigger picture of life. We have families, partners, homes, jobs, good things, not so good things … the whole gamut of life's emotions. Athletes and those that seek joy in the mountains are often just trying to find some sense and solid ground in what can be a crazy and confusing world.

I chose to follow the seasons when curating the images, beginning with winter and the often brutal Scottish winter climbing. The variety of Scottish terrain, weather and even weather patterns from year to year means that in any given season, any number of different sports may be possible, sometimes all in the same day. The flow of images reflects this amazing potential for outdoor adventures in this special country.

I hope in these pages you find fuel for your next Scottish adventure, the inspiration to pick up a camera the next time you go outdoors, or to take your children up a hill or go coasteering or mountain biking. Or maybe to get together with pals in a bar and come up with some crazy plan – which, when the effects of alcohol have worn off, might leave you wondering, 'what on earth were we thinking?' … but go ahead and do it anyway.

Let's celebrate the craziness, the brawn and the baws that make Scotland an adventure-sports paradise.

WINTER

« Adam MacKintosh ice climbing on a wet day on Ben Nevis.
We were hoping we would get below the freezing level
as we climbed higher.

THE HURTING

The Hurting at Coire an t-Sneachda in the Cairngorms is one of the hardest trad mixed routes in Scotland. First climbed by Dave MacLeod in 2005, and graded XI, 11, until 2015 it had seen less than a handful of repeats and by some of the best climbers in the world. This series of images is of Ines Papert, German ice climbing world champion, making the first female ascent and fifth ascent overall in what were horrendous conditions.

I had planned to meet Ines and her climbing partner, Simon Yearsley, in the car park at the Cairngorm ski centre at 6 a.m. in an attempt to beat a weather front that was expected to come in at 1 p.m. with predicted 100-mile-per-hour gusts. From the way Ines's campervan was being buffeted from side to side in the car park, it seemed the weather front had arrived early. Head down to the cafe for breakfast and have an easy day, I thought. I couldn't quite believe it when Ines and Simon said that as we were all here we might as well head up and look at the route as it might be sheltered from the wind. Scottish optimism at its best! I really couldn't see how this was going to work, but we walked in to the Fiacaill Buttress, being blown sideways by the wind and with visibility down to about fifteen metres due to the amount of snow falling and being blown around. Ines geared up, thankfully putting on brightly coloured clothing, and Simon put her on belay. I was on a rigging line alongside her and jumared up the rope to get the images.

It was -10 °C without wind chill, and the eyepiece, screen and camera controls were icing over as the moisture from my breath froze on to the camera. I had to keep clearing snow from the camera's eyepiece and the front element of the lens – seeing anything through the lens was a real effort – and trying to check if the images were sharp and make sure the autofocus wasn't focusing on the spindrift snow was a challenge. I had serious doubts about whether I would get anything usable from the day, and really hoped that I would get at least one image that represented the conditions and Ines's climb. I breathed a huge sigh of relief as Ines topped out.

Once we'd eventually headed down to the cafe and thawed out I was able to look at the images on the back of the camera.

'Do you think you got anything?' Ines asked, hopefully.

Feeling the tension in my body and mind relax, I replied, 'Yeah, I think there might be something here which will work.'

« Ines Papert repeating *The Hurting* (XI, 11) at Coire an t-Sneachda in the Cairngorms.

High winds and poor visibility are common during a day's climbing or walking in Scotland. This photo was shot on the same day as Ines's ascent of *The Hurting* and shows just how brutal conditions were.

Climbers battle against high winds on the east ridge of Càrn Mòr Dearg.

Graeme Douglas on *Central Gully Left* (II) in the Northern Corries on a typical Scottish day. Shot on commission for Glenmore Lodge.

Climbers ascending the west flank of Aonach Mòr on a bluebird day on the Nevis Range.

Blair Aitken skiing on the west flank of Aonach Mòr. »

Climbers walk up past icicles on the Waterslide Slab on the east flank of Buachaille Etive Mòr.

Abseiling down *Italian Right-Hand* on Ben Nevis.

Hunting the pow.

Canon EOS 5D Mark III, 24–105mm, ISO 800, 1/800, f16

Early on when I was working on this book I came to realise that you don't make just one plan in Scotland, you make several plans because there are so many factors that can change what you are able to do on any given day. On this particular December day I had planned to be shooting in the mountains, but heavy snowfall over the preceding days meant that the avalanche risk was high and until the snowpack had gone through a thaw/freeze cycle it was unsafe to head into the hills. So I made a last-minute call to a friend, and he suggested his son and his pals take the day off school to go snowboarding and get some images. If snow's up, take the day off school and go shred some lines – you can't argue with that!

On the day it was touch and go whether the wind would settle enough to allow the chairlifts to run, but eventually the lifts opened and we headed up the hill. It was windy, with spindrift blowing around, but the light was amazing as the sun was low in the sky. Being midwinter, even at midday the sun barely made it above the level of the mountain. As the boys were hiking back up the hill I saw this image. The snow was being blown towards the lens and it was difficult getting a shot that wasn't obscured by snow and ice – I was cleaning the lens with a tissue I had grabbed from one of the lift operators in between shots – and out of the dozen or so shots I took, only this one was clean enough to be usable. I was fortunate that it was included in the *Landscape Photographer of the Year* book in 2013.

Probably the most photogenic white-water river in Scotland. The Middle Etive lends itself to being photographed, especially the last big drop. Callum Anderson in action.

Big drops in Scotland don't come much bigger than Inchree »
Falls near Glencoe, and on this day Callum Anderson (pictured)
and Dave Biggins were running this fall for the first time.

Perfect conditions on Creag Meagcidh, with Max Cole in action on *Last Post* (V, 5).

THE RAIN

BY NICK BULLOCK

The rain … the bloody rain … it poured. And poured. And poured. The bloody permanent dark. The dark was smothering. Depressing. Invasive.

Through the day, I ran the narrow lonely lane from Roybridge that headed towards Glen Roy, undulating, winding. The rain bounced from the surface of the road. Ancient trees lined the lane and growing on their trunks was glowing moss. The brown peaty river – frothing white and bubbly – churned its twisting way around mossy boulders. Running, sweating, steaming. The deserted lay-by. Empty bottles – Glen's Vodka, J.P. Chenet Blanc – and discarded pink toilet paper, a soggy rosy pile. I imagined I was running along Cormac McCarthy's *The Road*. I felt separated in these post-apocalyptic highlands with only my thoughts for company. No one has a monopoly on misery …

I had walked into four different crags in the week and then walked out again. My rucksack remained unpacked. The most memorable and inspiring part of the week's failures had been the 5 a.m. battle to reach the Cairngorm plateau. Snow, gales, a white-out. What the fuck had Robbo and I been thinking?

In the beam of the head torch, I picked out a white carrier bag blowing in my direction. It was only when it tumbled nearer that I realised it was a ptarmigan, being beaten by the wind. Her wings, so used to being strong and carrying her body, flapped around like polythene. She clawed the snow with broad feathery legs and at last found purchase, hunkering about a metre away from me. My torch shone into her dark eyes, and they blazed.

Sitting in the Wetherspoons pub down the far end of Fort William High Street, the rain hit the outside of the windows. I stared at my laptop. After an aggressive email I decided no more. No more aggression. With a single 'send' my relationship was over. I felt alone.

Another day of rain. I sat in my van in Morrisons car park watching people leaving the train station and meeting loved ones. I sat and watched people embracing in the pouring rain. I wondered how long it would be before they hated each other and didn't speak.

Heading for the underpass towards Fort William town centre, I avoided the large puddles rippled by the wind. The waves on the surface of the puddles washed up on a beach of pavement. My mood was dark. It had been too long since the last numbing climb and waiting in wet Scotland made me miserable; I had too much time to think, I had too many conversations with myself. I was pitiful! I attempted to reason with myself. I attempted to see the truth and what was rational, but all I could see in the heavy drops of rain was loss.

Streams of water poured down the tiles on the front face of the underpass. The inside was lit, almost dazzling compared to the world outside. Music echoed and filtered begrudgingly into the damp gloom. The busker was in his fifties, a medium-sized man – wax jacket, bit of a belly, tweed flat cap, grey complexion and a worn and weary face.

He played an acoustic guitar and his singing and playing were good. Emotion stirred deep inside the pit of my stomach. *Why did he need to busk, what had gone wrong? Was he on his own?* His eyes were sharp, they stirred something in me – something that punched me in my hollow self-pitying gut. I placed a few coins in his guitar case and looked at him, deep into those eyes. Swinging the guitar from side to side – strumming and singing – he looked up and gave me a nod.

Walking from the underpass and back into the rain, my mood felt lighter. I made a pact with myself to stop wallowing in self-pity and to try to cheer up. There was always a glimmer of hope in the small unnoticed things of life, like a busker's nod.

I drove to Aviemore and Glenmore Lodge on Sunday and on Monday morning, the first day of the BMC Winter International Meet, the forecast was atrocious. What to do? My mood was once again sliding, but I thought of the busker, music, life, love and the ptarmigan. I decided that Jon Walsh – the Canadian climber I was partnered up with for the meet – and I should walk in to Creag Meggie just to check out conditions, put in a track and if it was anything like suitable, we would stash the gear ready for the following day – which had a slightly better forecast.

The following day Jon and I started walking in the dark. The snow fell in large wet flakes. And in the dark and the wind, the drifting snow filled *Raeburn's Gully* and sloughed from Pinnacle Buttress. Our tracks from the day before were only just visible as we approached our intended climb, a climb called *Extasy* that had only seen two previous ascents.

Raeburn's Gully felt dangerous with the massive amount of snow. As Jon and I geared up beneath the cliff that was covered with gobs of ice, I could not stop thinking of the time I had been here just over a year before with my girlfriend – the start of our relationship. '*Take me winter climbing.*' On that occasion we had climbed *Smith's Gully* and afterwards we had walked out in training shoes, chatting and excited to be in each other's company. It had been so warm. Little birds flitted in the trees and spring felt close.

Jon and I battled the snow and the difficult conditions, and later topped out after completing the third ascent of *Extasy*. Neither of us fancied crawling on to the plateau because the wind howled, driving the snow to white-out, so we abseiled until we stood on the Appollyon Ledge where we traversed to *Smith's Gully*. Immediately I recognised the belay where I had stood and watched her climb towards me just over a year ago – she had been so happy and full of life.

After the final day of the meet, when all of the visitors had gone, I decided to head south. I wanted to meet her and attempt to resurrect our relationship.

Loch Linnhe, the black pool, the sea loch that follows the great fault, was on my right. A fishing boat, strong, but so easy for the sea to wreck, rolled on the swell. Rusting angle iron covered in seaweed with bobbing car tyres and blue polypropylene. Bubbled brown scum washed up on to the pebbled shore. An oystercatcher with his long orange beak skittered amongst the green probing cockles. Dark clouds passed across the surface of the loch. A rain squall troubled. And beneath, hidden out of sight in the deep, the wrasse and whiting threaded the kelp while somehow maintaining their position amongst the cold currents.

Look down, look up …

I'm often struck by how much beauty is literally right under our feet if we take the time to look down, or above us if we look up at the trees and clouds. These shots were taken on the same day as the images of Creag Meagaidh on the previous pages and I took some time with a macro lens to photograph some of the ice formations on the river by the path.

Descending from the summit of Stob Coire nan Lochan in Glencoe after climbing *Crest Route*.

The stillness of the lochan in the coire.

Caspar McKeever on *Compression Crack* (V, 5), Ben Nevis.

Tom Livingstone and Uisdean Hawthorn on *Pic 'n' Mix* (VIII, 8), Coire an Lochain, Cairngorms.
I had abseiled in from a snow bollard in order to get the shot.

Mountain biking in Glenmore Forest. I had just returned from shooting for three days on the north face of Ben Nevis and some of the team at Glenmore Lodge decided they wanted an impromptu photographic workshop the following day. Graeme Hepburn in action.

Blair Aitken skiing *Yellow Belly* on Aonach Mòr with dramatic clouds over the Mamores.

The C.I.C. Hut, Scotland's only mountain hut, in full winter conditions.

A claggy day with the freezing level above the summits on the *Fiacaill Ridge* in the Northern Corries. Climber: Louisa Reynolds.

Mountain guide Ali Rose helping to evacuate a climber with a dislocated knee due to being caught in an avalanche.
Route choice is a big factor in staying safe in the mountains in winter.

ICE CLIMBING

BY DAVID CANNING

davecanning.wixsite.com/poetry

A lifetime divides us from the withered city,
aging, finite, accelerating;
time here expands to fill the space between our footsteps.

We tread with care the ice-cracked crust,
nylon thin, stretched across a lava heart,
kettled within a heaving caldera;

senses, pin-prick keen, surface and boil,
cold slaps like a midwife, as we
gulp at the milk-white air,

retreat glacially into the womb of the mountain
cast from the fontanelle of the earth:
newborn, grey-skinned and ready to gasp.

Suspended by umbilical ropes
we walk the water's winter-silenced rage,
a belayed cascade captured in the act of falling;

everything that before appeared certain and fixed,
melts, fuses, and re-forms around
arcing flows of hands and feet-

thought and instinct,
known and unknown,
seen and the unseen,

sensing and believing,
falling and ascending,
end and beginning

become as the wind is to the sky,
blood to the heartbeat,
gravity to the turning earth.

We will be old again in the time-kept city,
but the eternal mountain
lies like an ice splinter under the skin,

a flash in the corner of the eye,
a word caught on the tip of the tongue,
a thought frozen at the moment of its dreaming.

« Shot during a campaign capturing ice climbing on the cliffs of Ben Nevis. Using wide-angle lenses there is a risk that the lens changes the apparent gradient of the climb. Trying to capture steepness when looking straight up or down a route is difficult and I try and keep the climber and cliff edge nearest the edge of the frame parallel to the frame to avoid the convergence of lines.

Raised footprints, a form of sastrugi, created from the compacted snow remaining after the softer snow has been blown away.

Climbers heading up towards *The Curtain*, Ben Nevis.

The North East Buttress of Ben Nevis.

« Inside the C.I.C. Hut. Sometimes it's the little details that really help to tell a story and work well alongside the more 'extreme' images of adventure sports.

Sunrise and icicles on Ben Nevis.

High winds on the path down from the C.I.C. Hut. Just before taking this image one of the team had said to me, 'You might as well put the camera away – you're not going to get anything now'. I actually think that when conditions are extreme and the winds are gusting up to 100 miles per hour, the potential to get an image that tells a story is much better than on a bluebird day.

Sam Owens on *The Vent* (II) at Coire an Lochain in the Cairngorms.

Dave Biggins on the River Coe, Glencoe.

CRÈME DE VIOLETTE

BY TOM LIVINGSTONE

Driving on the left side of the road – the *right* side of the road – Ben and I chipped away at the everlasting drive. Slowly, very slowly, we crept north, the satnav centred over Torridon. The North West Highlands: the crème de la crème of Scottish winter climbing? 'A high-pressure system's in the area,' Ben said with excitement. 'It's going to be mint. There're so many routes to do, and I think the North West is in!'

I admitted I didn't really know what was going on. Three days after landing back in the country, my mind was still on Canadian time. I'd only seen glimpses of the Scottish season so far. I replaced my phone's quick links: hello again, MWIS forecasts.

'What's the plan, Ben?' I asked between driving stints. In recent winters, Scotland's climbing season had been found wanting, so I was keen to make up for lost time.

Thankfully, Ben held everything in control: 'Beinn Eighe tomorrow, Beinn Bhàn the day after,' he said quietly.

I'd only tied in a few times with Ben, and they'd been enjoyable, stress-free experiences. The previous summer in North Wales we'd dodged rain showers, Ben confirming the stories I'd heard. The strongest memory was Ben's smooth ascent of *Lord of the Flies* (E6 6a).

We drove north, hour after hour. It was long past my bedtime, regardless of which time zone I was in. It felt like the day had closed long ago, too. Darkness had set in, like a heavy blanket on the Scottish moorland. Rain turned to sleet, then to snow, then back to rain again.

Suddenly, the van headlights picked up a pair of ghostly grey eyes by the side of the road. *What the hell is that?* my brain screamed, wide awake. My foot instantly hovered over the brake. A second later, a stag picked its way towards the roadside, fully illuminated. Just before stepping on to the tarmac it paused, casually. It seemed oblivious of our impending collision, the van charging at sixty miles per hour, and me now jumping on the brakes. Instead, it turned slightly as if to say, 'get tae!' It was good to be back to Scotland. Even the animals did whatever they cared.

Tuesday. Beinn Eighe was all to ourselves. As we punched steps up the hillside, night slowly faded, like the turning of a dimmer switch. Instead of day breaking, we felt darkness release its grip, give up, allow brightness to seep into the world. Light arrived without real colour. Monochrome, lunar grey and black. Dark clouds, faint white mountains, bleak glens. But the scenery was still stunning in its own Scottish way, and the plateau near the summit gave us rare views of the Atlantic and the bulk of Liathach.

In between the wind, the spindrift and the bare landscape, we stood. Still. After the gusts, we snatched a moment of calm on the plateau. I breathed deeply and felt my lungs cool as I inhaled. We continued to the catchily named West Central Wall.

The climbing on West Central Wall is steep and intimidating, and the routes usually follow grooves and corners. You get the impression the first ascensionists searched for the obvious lines, climbing the weaknesses in these fortress walls. Grooves and corners tend to be friendly, all bridging, twice the footholds, and hopefully there's a friendly crack in the back. The luck runs out when you reach an impasse, usually a fat 'end-of-the-line-buddy' type of roof, and the route is forced left or right, away from the comfort of the corner, and on to an arête. *Shoot the Breeze* is a classic example – although I bet the first ascensionists were looking for this kind of adventure! Wild moves, the exposure suddenly at your heels, moving further and further away from gear … hopefully, though, the sanctuary of another corner is reached.

I think Ben chose *Crème de Violette* as our route for the day, and I enjoyed being in relative ignorance as we geared up. I recognised the name, but couldn't remember anything about it, which – in climbing – can be a bit like going into a boxing match with an undercover heavyweight world champion. Sometimes the stories, rumours and descriptions I hear make me more hesitant; sometimes, the hardest part is actually getting on the route. This time, however, ignorance was bliss, and I just assumed the worst: I assumed it'd be nails. *Oh right, cool,* I thought. *I'm sure this'll be hard, run-out and scary* … This approach usually works, and I'm therefore often pleasantly surprised to find gear and holds.

Ben did tell me one thing about the route to prepare me: Nick Bullock's comments on his and

Tim Neill's first ascent. Of the crux second pitch, Nick had said, 'Carefully pull right around the roof and climb the even more committing groove above (without thinking about where the last piece of gear was or even what the last piece of gear was).'

After Ben had led the first pitch, I set off up the second. Blue skies occasionally flashed overhead – a rarity for Scotland. The crag was almost 'over-rimed,' so I spent a lot of time searching for holds and gear, testing every placement. I hammered in kit regularly, aware of an imminent crux and run-out. This was the point where the comfort of a groove and corner ended, the large roof above blocking further progress. *Here goes*, I thought, and started teetering towards the arête …

At the belay, forty metres above Ben, I remember reflecting after a long and testing pitch.

My experiences on *Crème de Violette* might be totally different to others. Climbing is so subjective; it's a personal experience, and there's no comparison or competition. And Scottish winter is perhaps the most subjective of all types of climbing. I could say, 'the gear was all there and the hooks were pretty good'. But actually, my comments are pointless because my experience is only my interpretation.

Nick might've been a bit gripped, thinking he was on a massive sandbag of an VIII, 8 called *Bruised Violet*. He might've missed gear. It might've been a bit of a shock, the crack could have been verglassed, there could have been loose rock …

I remember talking to Uisdean about *The Secret*. He was fresh back from Indian Creek and described the route as 'straightforward'. Although he'd climbed the main pitch on second, he'd still found plenty of good jams all the way. I'd found it steady, but with spindrift constantly washing down the crag, heavy gusts and some verglassed rock, it was quite a battle at times. I was initially quick to counter Uisdean's comments, but then again: Scottish winter climbs vary from day to day. Our experiences on the route vary minute to minute.

You might as well forget the grade because you'll be colder/warmer, fitter/weaker, more/less experienced and lucky/unlucky compared to everyone else that's climbed the route. The rock might be verglassed or the cracks dug out or the rime purely cosmetic or your belayer's doing the death shiver … In fact, you might as well forget about other people's experiences and comments, because you're going to have your own adventure, regardless!

Perhaps I was well prepared from a month of mixed climbing in Canada, but thankfully I found Nick's comments didn't match with my time on *Crème de Violette*. Nonetheless, he'd had the first-ascent experience, and he didn't know what he might find on the other side of the roof. I think his comments don't exactly insinuate that it's run-out or that the gear's poor, but there's plenty of implication. But then again, who knows, and who cares – it's just climbing! Besides, our ascent doesn't count anyway. I think, looking at the photos

afterwards, I belayed higher than Nick did. We also exited a metre left of Nick and Tim's final pitch, after Ben tried the 'direct' finish and then I looked round the corner … So, good effort to Nick and Tim for putting it up in the first place. I've been meaning to get back to Beinn Eighe for some new route ideas, but talk is cheap and I'm still not in Scotland.

The following day was equally rewarding, as we climbed *The God Delusion* (IX, 9) on Beinn Bhàn, getting the 'full' Scottish experience … But that's another story. Thanks for a good couple of days, Ben.

The bulk of Aonach Eagach glimpsed through the mist.

THE CHOICE

BY ELANA BADER

The ground crumbles beneath my feet, vanishing.
I am at once suspended, and falling.

The choice is mine:
Bow to the dark void of fear,
and fall deeper, or
Look up to the horizon,
and step over the threshold.

I am at once decided,
and frozen.
The choice is mine.

« Rebecca Coles climbing *White Shark* (IV, 4) on the east face of Aonach Mòr.

Kev Shields on *Fast and Furious* (M10) at Newtyle Quarry.

« Joe Saunders, British dry-tooling champion, on *DTS Spirit* (M12)
   at the steep Newtyle Quarry near Dunkeld.

MAKING DECISIONS

BY MIKE PESCOD

In 2004 I made a decision to do some ice climbing under developing cornices on Aonach Mòr. Of course, a cornice collapsed and triggered an avalanche above me. I had climbed about thirty metres and was placing anchors for a belay when it hit me and carried me all the way back to the bottom of the climb.

I broke vertebrae T12, L2 and L3 in my back, my pelvis, an ankle and some ribs. The people I was with were brilliant and called 999 immediately. There were rescue team members very close at hand working at Nevis Range ski area and two of them came down Easy Gully to find me. A third team member went back to get some more equipment but was blown off the top of the crag and fell 100 metres. He was so lucky because he landed literally at the feet of the first two guys who were able to help him straight away. It took a couple of hours to get him on a stretcher and hauled up to the ski area so it was five hours before anyone came round to me. By this time the weather was terrible. It was a really difficult job getting me out, taking something like three hours.

In the Belford Hospital that night I was in a bed next to the guy who had been blown off the crag. We looked at each other and kind of shrugged, 'well that's how it goes sometimes'.

I was in hospital in Glasgow for nearly six weeks so I had plenty of time to analyse what had gone wrong. To start with I put it down to being in the wrong place at the wrong time: I was just unlucky. If I did exactly the same thing again, I thought, I would not get avalanched. It was just a one in ten or one in 100 chance. But, if that was the case, for every day I went climbing, whether or not I came home would just be down to luck. That would be no way to live and work. I couldn't have the future of my career and my family reliant on good luck.

So instead I looked at all the small decisions that led me to be there at that time, and there was a list of human factors that led me all the way there. I had a good plan at the start of the day that I should have stuck to, but I changed the plan for a number of reasons: meeting at Nevis Range and only discussing the plan on the gondola ride when we were committed to going up Aonach Mòr; rescheduling the second day and therefore wanting to get a bit more out of this first day; being new to guiding and the feeling that I had to deliver something special no matter what; the clear desire of my clients to climb this bit of ice; familiarity with the climb since I had climbed it a week previously. None of these things had anything to do with the snow in front of me which was clearly telling me not to climb the route.

More recently, with more and more experience, I am far more comfortable making decisions based on the conditions, even if that means my clients are disappointed. Having been guiding full-time in Scotland for fifteen years I think I am better able to make good decisions more of the time, but you always have to focus on what you are doing and be very aware of the human factors that lead us to make poor decisions. You have to be able to say, 'No, not today', even if someone else goes right past you and does it. That person might have just survived a fifty-fifty chance and be completely unaware of it.

« Seeking out an ice line on a claggy day on Ben Nevis.

Mike Pescod, owner of Abacus Mountain Guides and author of the Cicerone guidebook, *Winter Climbs Ben Nevis and Glen Coe*.

Italian Right-Hand (IV, 4), Ben Nevis.

« Mike Pescod on *Compression Crack* (V, 5), Ben Nevis. We chose the central line to climb as I thought it may give us the most photogenic shots. In this image of Mike, his green jacket works well with the green rope and there was a brief break in the clouds allowing a touch of blue sky on an otherwise cloudy and windy day. I shouted up to Mike to put his left leg out to the side as I felt the combination of leg and arm movement would give a better composition. It was only when I followed him up the route that I realised how off balance that actually must have felt.

Canon EOS 5D Mark III, 24–70mm, ISO 800, 1/1000, f11

Goggles are de rigueur in the high winds often found on the Cairngorm plateau.
This shot was taken during a Glenmore Lodge winter skills course.

Sally Hudson of Abacus Mountain Guides during a winter climbing photoshoot.

ONE DAY

BY ELANA BADER

I want to believe
that I can return
these dying parts of me
back to the Earth,
gratefully,

and that they will return
in a new season,
one day,
vibrant and alive once again.

« Walking down the Allt a' Mhuilinn by Ben Nevis. This image was shot as part of the Ellis Brigham winter shoot in 2017. I had previsualised a shot with the river and the bulk of Càrn Mòr Dearg showing through the mist and we waited for a while for the mists to lift slightly so we could see some of the bulk of the mountain in the background. I used a 70–200mm lens to get some compression of the background and foreground and experimented with the amount of river to incluce. As it was raining, the long lens hood gave it good protection from water droplets on the front element, and shooting at 1/1000 second helped to minimise the effect of wind buffeting and camera shake. I carry the lightest of the Canon 70–200mm lenses in the mountains: the f4 version instead of the heavy f2.8.

Early morning on the Bidean nam Bian massif in Glencoe.

Ski tourers in early morning mist at Glenshee in the Cairngorms.

SPRING

« Ian Sherrington bootpacking up the slopes
above Coire an Lochain, Cairngorms.

Louise Anna on the trail up to Ben Alder. A lot of Scottish mountain biking involves hike-a-bike to access some of the best and most remote trails.

Connor Skinner mountain biking in Glen Nevis with Steall Falls in the background.

Breathtaking views into the corries of Ben Alder, one of the finest mountain-bike tours in Scotland.

Blair Aitken on the steep entrance to *Number Five Gully* on Ben Nevis.

Peter MacKenzie skis *South Castle Gully*, Ben Nevis.

Peter MacKenzie on *Arch Gully*, Ben Nevis.

The 'cans not cams' tour – the best steep skiers in Scotland skiing the gully lines of Ben Nevis. Peter on *Ledge Route* with a ginger beer can instead of a cam (*top left*), and negotiating the large chockstone in *Arch Gully*. (Note that cans are not acceptable forms of rock protection and this image was taken as a joke!)

On this weekend in 2017 I had planned to be ski touring, but many will remember this year as being a very bad year for snow and we ended up photographing mountain biking above Kinlochleven instead in an attempt to salvage the day.

Climbers on the Northern Pinnacles of Liathach.

Beinn Eighe in a hailstorm.

Early spring snow on the Goat Track, Coire an t-Sneachda.

Sally Hudson on *Italian Right-Hand* (IV, 4), Ben Nevis. »

« Max Willcocks and Steph Ede bootpacking into the Northern Corries before zero visibility stopped play.

Setting up an abseil at Cummingston.

COMPOSITION

There is a lot of information out there about composition and what makes a shot 'work'. I once said during one of my courses at Glenmore Lodge that the rule of thirds is a load of rubbish, which brought gasps of disbelief from my course attendees. What I meant was that it's not the be all and end all of compositional ideas; there's a lot more to composition than simply applying a formula to a scene and voila, you have an amazing image.

An image has to be the vessel for an emotional message, and that message has to connect with the viewer in a heartbeat, to draw them in and engage them. And the emotion has to come from within the photographer. To my mind, photography is both an art and a craft: it can simply record and document something – a place in time, a building, or simply historical facts, but the *art* of photography is to move someone to feel what you felt when you pressed the shutter. Very occasionally I have experienced a physical sensation in my gut when I've been taking photographs. It might have been a coming together of elements, a fleeting shaft of light or shadow, or a body position – something that was almost too quick for my conscious mind to respond to but which my subconscious registered, and when I've gone back and looked at the images I've found something special.

In my lectures I often talk of the art of pre-visualisation – imagining in your mind what sort of images you are looking for, imagining how that would feel, what the angles and backdrop would look like, how the wind would look on the elements and what the light and shadows would be doing. I also like to think of the technical things: would I need strobes? How many? What aperture and shutter speed would I want to work with? This can be viewed as setting an intention as to what you want the shoot to deliver, and it's a useful exercise to undertake prior to any given shoot.

Of course, you can't predict the weather and conditions so precisely that you know exactly what the light and shadows will be doing on a particular day, but having blueprints in your mind is a great way of developing your own compositional ideas. And then, when you are out and about and things do start to happen, the magic begins to spark in your brain and connections and images start to take shape.

Balance is important in images. The rule of thirds is certainly one way to find balance, but I like to *feel* the balance rather than use a formula, so often I'll balance textures and use opposite corners in images and frequently strong diagonals to position the main subject where I *feel* it works best.

People say that if you can climb safely on Ben Nevis in winter then you can probably climb anywhere in the world. There is a lot of truth in that. Many top alpinists have learned their skills on the Ben and have gone on to do some of the hardest routes in the world. The same may be true for photography: some of the harshest conditions you can experience without going to polar extremes or the greater ranges can be found on Ben Nevis or in the Northern Corries – high winds, zero visibility and wind chill of below -10 °C. Getting usable images in these conditions is hard and having blueprints in your mind enables you to work efficiently and quickly to get the images and tell the story you want. Developing the craft of photography, practising it and trying different compositional ideas then frees your mind to focus on the art of image making in difficult conditions.

Certain lenses can lend themselves to different compositional ideas. For example, Canon's 17–40mm full-frame-equivalent wide-angle lens is great for working with a central-themed composition, as in the image of Tom and Uisdean on the front cover of this book. Because of its wide coverage, it's a great lens for pulling in lots of lines and really using them as lead-in lines for your main subject.

I often describe photography as the art of subtraction – what you choose to leave out of the frame is as important as what you choose to include. The fact is, we are presenting a small portion of the landscape or action to create an image and message that we want to portray, and less is definitely more in images. I try to minimise the number of elements within a photograph to allow the image to speak clearly rather than having too many elements conflicting with one another. I will often exclude elements from the frame to simplify the image and its message, to reduce it down to its core: hence, the art of subtraction.

Colin Meek and Lee Fleming trail running on and around the beautiful An Teallach, Wester Ross.

Dramatic skies and light on Sgùrr an Fheadain, the Cuillins, Isle of Skye. Climbers: Matt Barrett and Scott Brooks.

James Dunn on the trails around the Scottish Border town of Peebles, home to some of the best riding in the country.

Blizzard conditions in the Northern Corries.

« James Hatfield on an early morning blast down
   Janet's Brae at Glentress with a spring dusting of snow.

Callum Anderson on the Middle Etive.

Pinnacle Ridge of Sgùrr nan Gillean Isle of Skye.

Highland cattle on the road to Elgol, Isle of Skye.

« Guy Stevens and Lee Fleming on Sgùrr Alasdair, Isle of Skye. Guy, Lee and I were on Skye for a few days and the plan was to get some shots on the ridge. The weather was typical Skye but the forecast was for the occasional break in the cloud and rain. On the day I took this shot, we had sheltered in one of the caves on the way up to Sgùrr Alasdair while the rains passed. After having a brew and sitting it out for forty minutes or so, we headed up. I had previsualised a shot I wanted to get and felt the fisheye would give me the wide sweep I wanted, looking down into the corries and capturing some sense of the drama and beauty of the place. I'm glad it wasn't a bluebird day as the clouds give the image some drama and it's more typically Scottish.

Canon EOS 5D Mark III, 8–15mm fisheye, ISO 400, 1/400, f11

Lee Fleming on *Jamie Jampot* (VS 4c) on the cliffs of Suidhe Biorach near Elgol, Isle of Skye.

The Fairy Pools, Glen Brittle, Isle of Skye. A magnet for tourists and midges in the summer.

Sgùr nan Gillean, Isle of Skye: (*above*) Climbers on the ledge traverse on Pinnacle Ridge;
(*right*) Jon Jones, head of mountaineering at Glenmore Lodge, on the West Ridge.

SUMMER

« Aonach Eagach, Glencoe.

Runners on and around An Teallach, Wester Ross.

Paul Tattersall in evening light on Jetty Crag near Gruinard Bay in the North West Highlands. We had been out all day and it had rained all day. We had planned to get images on Stac Pollaidh but it had been a washout and on the drive back to Poolewe we passed Jetty Crag; finally we had the light we had been waiting for.

Joe Saunders on *Grey Panther* (E1 5b), Kilt Rock, Isle of Skye.

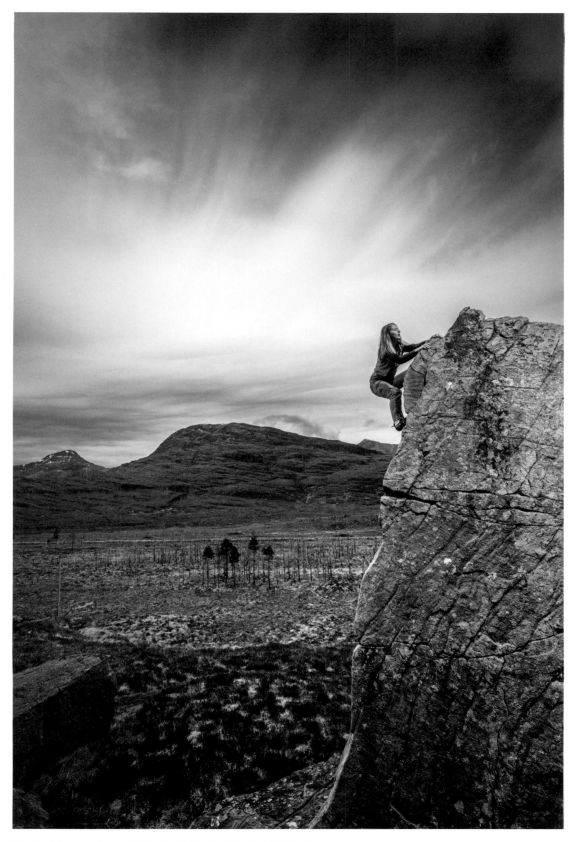

Heather Osborne on *Layback Arête* (Font 4+) on the Celtic Boulder, Torridon.

I had hoped to be coming down the west flank of Beinn Eighe a bit »
later in the day to catch the sun lower in the sky. The question then was:
do we wait and potentially get swarmed by midges and miss
last orders for food back in Torridon, or do we accept that we've
had a good day, get the shot and head down to get food … ?

Canon EOS 5D Mark IV, 24–70mm, ISO 800, 1/1600, f11

FEELING CONNECTED

There's no escaping it now, for better or worse, getting likes and followers is almost as important to a photographer as getting high-quality images. And the number of followers you have on Instagram and Facebook doesn't necessarily bear any relation to how good your images are. It's a PR exercise, and the more savvy you can be at manipulating social media, the more followers you'll have. But is a phone or tablet screen the best place to consume art? Our attention span is so short now with images on our feeds daily, that an image which could inspire and capture our imagination is only there for a fleeting moment before it's gone from our consciousness.

I do think that we lose a connection with art when it's only viewed online. There is an extra dimension when it's printed and we can hold it in our hands, or hang it on our wall as a thing of contemplation; the images can bring their own energy to a space.

With landscape and adventure-sports images, part of the emotional response that inspires the photographer is that you are surrounded by this immense landscape and you are just a tiny part of it. And part of that feeling can't really be conveyed unless the image is printed out in a size that conveys that emotion. When the first *Landscape Photographer of the Year* book came out I was completely blown away by the richness and depth of the images to the extent that I could only really look at a handful of images in one sitting; it was too intense for me at that time. I don't think the experience would have been the same if I was viewing the images on my phone.

How many couples keep their wedding day photos on only their phone or tablet? Maybe a few, but the majority will print them and either put them in an album or have a number of them displayed on walls: they are important photographs and having a physical image to hold is part of the psychological and emotional connection with the moment captured in the image. I encourage you, if you have a number of images that mean something to you, to get them printed for your own photobook or to frame them for your wall.

ARE YOU?

BY ELANA BADER

We are bound to each other,
None of us an island,
Dependent on connection
To survive and thrive,

Grounded only by the constancy of
Earth beneath our feet
True nourishment for
Our human fragility.

Are you captive in the digital expectations
Of an illusionary self,
Deluded by who you ought to be?

Those screens, angles and rigid sides
We have framed
As our only acceptable living space,
Our eyes focussed on the smallest of spaces
In this vast, rich world of ours.

The constancy of change
Is not eternal.
These moments are of their last
Knowing that chaos is to come.

Saying a goodbye, grieving for what we'll lose,
As we stand by, unable to turn back time
Or undo our mistakes of the past
Of over-inflated egos,

The shared human condition
Untapped and unshared.

Isolation and captivity
Driving us all insane,
Polluted minds and hearts
Souls boxed into routine
And schedule,

Separated and ill-equipped
Whilst our life source
Dies, gasping under the
Weight of our ignorant presence.

Detached from our source,
Lost in a technological headspace
Deconditioned to our origins
Shying away.

How was it not enough?
We're more starved,
More deprived than ever.

Quick bursts of attention
Dominate hasty dopamine hits
Always looking for that next fix
Brains out of breath,
Opinionated, not educated.

Heather Csborne on *East Buttress* (Diff), Beinn Eighe.

Steve Perry on *Skyeman* (E2 5b), Kilt Rock, Isle of Skye.

Heather Osborne on *A Fistful of Dollarite* (E1 5b), Neist Point, Isle of Skye.

The focus on *Road to Ruin* (E2 5b), Kilt Rock, Isle of Skye.

Even ng bouldering session in Coire Lagan, Isle of Skye.

Squelch (Font 6c) on the Ship Boulder, Torridon.

An evening bouldering session in Torridon beneath fiery skies.

David Murray mountain biking in Torridon on a wet and windy day. On clear days the views around the trails here are stunning – not on this day though!

Biking through snow patches around Ben Alder.

« Mountain bikers Alastair McLennan Snr, Alastair McLennan Jnr and Keir Coupland enjoy last light on Beinn Fhada. This photograph was taken on the first day of shooting for *Extreme Scotland* back in July 2012 and was one of the first images I took with the Canon EOS 5D Mark III which I had just bought to work alongside my 5D Mark II. I always try and carry two full-frame bodies when I go away on a trip so that if one fails I always have a backup camera. I had swapped T-shirts with Alastair Snr before this shot as I thought the continuity of colour with the riders and the foreground grass added something to the shot. This image sums up what my idea for the *Extreme Scotland* project was – and is – all about: great athletes, great light and a great landscape to work with.

Canon EOS 5D Mark III, 70–200mm, ISO 800, 1/1000, f4

Keir Coupland and Alastair McLennan Jnr riding down the Allt a' Mhuilinn below Ben Nevis.

Lawrence Hughes on *Rehab Roof* (F7b) at Glutton Crag near Ullapool.

« Ross Creber climbing at Logie Head in Aberdeenshire.

The fence, Wester Ross.

Murdoch Jamieson on *Fun Prow* (F8a), Goat Crag, Wester Ross.

Paul Tattersall on the Cuillin Ridge during filming for Rab's new MeCo base layer in 2014.

Climbers descending into Coire Lagan, Isle of Skye.

« Colin Meek running on Beinn Alligin during a shoot for *Trail Running* magazine in 2013. For this image, I used the Elinchrom Quadra system hyper-synced to enable the use of shutter speeds faster than the camera's native sync speed, which allowed me to shoot directly into the sun and still have a well-lit subject.

Canon EOS 5D Mark III, 17–40mm, ISO 800, 1/800, f16, and Elinchrom Quadra with Pocket Wizard triggers

'After the Deluge', inspired by J.M.W. Turner's dramatic skies. Colin Meek running on Beinn Alligin.

Chris Prescott jumaring up the overhanging face of Dumbarton Rock to film James Pearson on *Rhapsody*.

James Pearson bouldering on the Dumbarton boulders in preparation for climbing *Rhapsody*.

Caroline Ciavaldini on the steep and technical *Requiem* (E8 6b) at Dumbarton Rock.

Evening light on Aonach Dubh, Glencoe.

The bridge over the River Etive on the A82 under the watchful eye of Buachaille Etive Mòr.

AUTUMN

« Georgina Maxwell biking amidst autumn colours in the Cairngorms.

Robbie Phillips on – and off – *Wild at Heart* (E7 6b) on The Cobbler, Arrochar.

Top: Walking into Kilt Rock on Isle of Skye.
Bottom: Guy Stevens on Kilt Rock's classic route *Grey Panther* (E1 5b) – an *Extreme Rock* tick.

Running on the Vertical Kilometer in the Mamores, part of the Skyline Scotland running series.

« An early start on Pinnacle Ridge, Sgùrr nan Gillean, Isle of Skye. It was our fourth day on Skye and limbs were tired, but I wanted to photograph Pinnacle Ridge. The last day had a lot of rain forecast from midday onwards so we made a 6 a.m. start from Sligachan and were well on to the ridge by 7.30 a.m. But, as is the way in Scotland, the rain arrived earlier than forecast and we had a soggy ascent of Pinnacle Ridge and descent down the west ridge.

Canon EOS 5D Mark III, 17–40mm, ISO 800, 1/80, f10

Georgina Maxwell crosses a river during a photography workshop in the Cairngorms.

« Paul Tattersall on the upper tier of Creag nan Luch, Poolewe.

Jake Thompsett and Jon Gupta running the coastal trails around Old Wick Castle, Caithness.

« Steve Macdonald running on Beinn a'Chrulaiste, Glencoe.

Jake Thompsett and Jon Gupta watching and waiting in Thurso for conditions to improve.

Surfing in Thurso in fine evening light.

These two birds seem to sum up the atmosphere of waiting around in Thurso during heavy seas and storms.

« Jake heading back to the van to defrost after a chilly session on the waves.

Rannoch Moor – beauty and destruction. I was trying to find an image on Rannoch Moor that wasn't the same as all the other images of the Black Mount and the lochans: there are thousands of images of that composition and I couldn't see the point of taking the exact same image that had been done so many times before. My eye was drawn to these cut tree stumps, and the moss and clouds together all made for a moody image that I think captures something of the feel of the place.

TOUCHING ROCK

BY ELANA BADER

Look at him, that guardian Shepherd
of the Valley.
He's calling me; can't you hear?

So I go to him, open to his moods
and his mind-games,
willing.

Immersed in his rock,
my polluted mind gives way
to find simple focus:

the air may whip around me,
taunting fear,
verticality tugging at my ease,

but I am elemental,
wild in my soul and
infused w th delicious joy.

« Elana Bader on the final pitch of *Agag's Groove* (V Diff)
on the Rannoch Wall of Buachaille Etive Mòr, Glencoe.

Running down Beinn a'Chrulaiste on a wet day in Glencoe.

On the road out to Mallaig one autumnal day, I stopped to take a walk through the woods and trees. I love the effect that backlighting has on water droplets and ice particles.

Descending from the summit of Buachaille Etive Mòr on a magical autumn evening. Spending a day like this in Scotland climbing a classic route with friends is truly special. The grades don't matter: it's the shared experience and being in such amazing places that counts.

Textures balance with one another on the final slope to the summit of Buachaille Etive Mòr with Elana and Sarah.

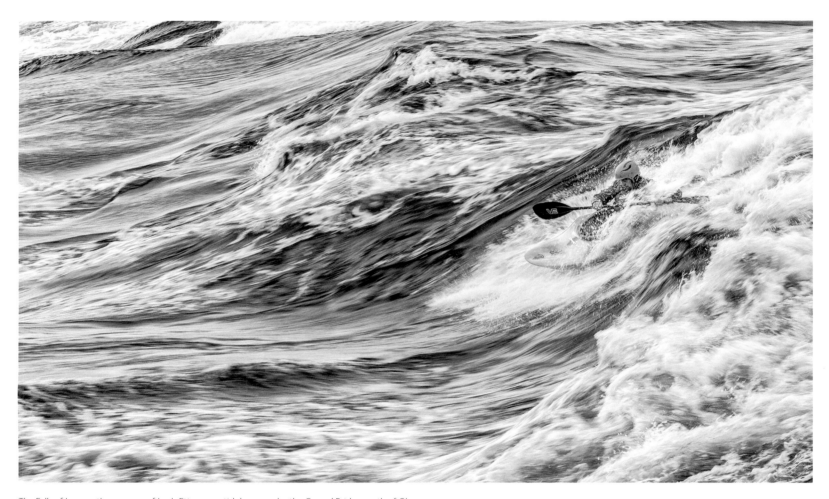

The Falls of Lora on the narrows of Loch Etive are a tidal race under the Connel Bridge north of Oban.
The flow changes over the course of the tide and many paddlers take two separate boats: a longer boat
for the early part of the flow, and a play boat for when the level has dropped enough to hold one.

« The last big drop on the River Nevis.

James Hatfield biking down Ben Lomond.

« Colin Meek running in Wester Ross. In 2014 I was filming *The Forge* (*vimeo.com/98953703*) and we were shooting all around the *An Teallach* and Fisherfield mountains. This is a still photograph taken during the film shoot with Colin. I was fortunate to have *The Forge* included in the Kendal Mountain Festival and in the 'Best of Kendal' world tour 2014.

Sgùrr a' Ghreadaidh.

COIRE 'N UAIGNEIS

BY STUART B. CAMPBELL

This is where you start
to become grounded:
drink deep from the quoich
of the coire; time begins
to exist elsewhere; the world recedes,
only the rock remains.
Touch the hard black scab
where, pulse beat after slow pulse beat,
the earth once bled out.
Under Bidein Druim nan Ramh,
brooding, loosing yourself
to find the way, the means;
that rhythm, a ripple gestating
within; the wounding hurt
healing, the scar-tissue gift of gabbro.

… and from this coire of solitude
Eoin og commits himself to the moves
with the grace of a stag, the impossible flow
of gravity becoming spent, like snowflakes
falling upwards. For him, for us, this moment
is without parallel, all the here and now
there ever is; and yet always
it is as if MacGill-eain mór was still
on Rassay to remind us
that this remains a future unknown
place; though Murray knew
balance and rhythm, heard in utter silence
more of the world's song,
one day alone at Sligachan he saw
in his reflection the physical
limitations of age; and how this,
too, is a kind of giving.

« Paul Tattersall below King's Chimney on the Cuillin Ridge,
Isle of Skye. Shot as part of the 2013 Rab MeCo base layer
campaign. The film shot as part of the campaign
is available on Vimeo: *vimeo.com/113787546*

Gavin Mackenzie running in Glencoe.

Looking down as climbers ascend Sgùrr an Fheadain, Isle of Skye.

Paul Tattersall on *Buena Vista* (E2 5b) at Loch Tollaidh Crags.

Paul Tattersall on the upper tier of Creag nan Luch.

ACKNOWLEDGEMENTS

I am indebted to all the athletes who have given their time, effort and expertise to make this book happen. It's a tribute to the Scottish outdoor community that so many of the people that are instrumental in making things happen in Scotland have been hugely supportive of this project and helped to make it become a reality.

In no particular order, thanks to: Derek Bain, Ines Papert, Simon Yearsley, Ali Rose, Adam MacKintosh, Sally Hudson, Mike Pescod, Graeme Douglas, Gavin Mackenzie, Blair Aitken, Mark Chadwick, Frazer Coupland, Keir Coupland, Alastair MacLennan Jnr, Alastair MacLennan Snr, Callum Anderson, Dave Biggins, Max Cole, Joe Saunders, Kev Shields, Graeme Hepburn, Louisa Reynolds, Jon Jones, Giles Trussell, Glenmore Lodge, Sam Owens, Tom Livingstone, Uisdean Hawthorn, Rebecca Coles, Louisa Anna, James Hatfield, Peter Mackenzie, Caspar McKeever, Heather Osborne, Elana Bader, Stephanie Ede, Colin Meek, Lee Fleming, Matt Barrett, James Dunn, Guy Stevens, Paul Tattersall, Steve Perry, David Murray, Ross Creber, Lawrence Hughes, Murdoch Jamieson, James Pearson, Caroline Ciavaldini, Robbie Phillips, Olly Bowman, Georgina Maxwell, Steve Macdonald, Jake Thompsett, Jon Gupta, Scott Brooks, Alex Parmenter, Sarah Gingell, Kirk Watson, Nick Bullock, Stuart B. Campbell, Connor Skinner and David Canning.

Please feel free to email me if you have any questions or comments about *Extreme Scotland*: **info@nadirkhan.co.uk**

If you're interested in developing your own photography, I run workshops based at Glenmore Lodge in the Cairngorms as well as one-to-one sessions by arrangement. We cover all aspects of photography and have a lot of fun with it. Please do get in touch.

@nadirkhanphotography
/nadirkhanphotography
/nadirkhan

www.nadirkhan.co.uk